# The Waters Under the Earth

Robert Siegel

canonpress
Moscow, Idaho

Also by Robert Siegel

*The Beasts and the Elders*
*In a Pig's Eye*
*Alpha Centauri*
*Whalesong*
*The Kingdom of Wundle*
*White Whale*
*The Ice at the End of the World*

Published by Canon Press
P.O. Box 8729, Moscow, ID 83843
800-488-2034 | www.canonpress.com

Robert Siegel, *The Waters Under the Earth*
Copyright © 2005 by Robert Siegel

Painting by Janet Siegel Rogers, *Seeing Beyond, Series XVIII,*
copyright © 2004 by Janet Siegel Rogers
Cover design by Paige Atwood

Printed in the United States of America.

*Library of Congress Cataloging-in-Publication Data*

Siegel, Robert
  The waters under the earth / Robert Siegel.
     p. cm.
  ISBN-13: 978-1-59128-030-9 (pbk.)
  ISBN-10: 1-59128-030-3 (pbk.)
  I. Title.
  PS3569.I382W38 2005

                                             2005001630

10 11 12 13 14 15 16          9 8 7 6 5 4 3 2

# The Waters Under the Earth

For Ann

# Contents

## Acknowledgments

Grateful acknowledgment is made to the following journals and anthologies in which some of the following poems were first published: *The Atlantic, Prairie Schooner, The Sewanee Review, Ploughshares, Image, Books & Culture, The Kansas Quarterly The Little Magazine, Arts & Letters, The Cream City Review, Cresset, The Wisconsin Academy Review, Midland Review, America, First Things, The Wisconsin Review, The Soil is Suited to the Seed, Motiv, The Christian Century, Poems for a Small Planet: Contemporary American Nature Poetry, Contemporary Poetry of New England,* and *The Generation of 2000: Contemporary American Poets.*

The author is also grateful to the University of Wisconsin-Milwaukee for several grants that contributed to the writing of these poems.

Last, he wishes to thank his editor, Douglas Jones, his friends, Robert Barth, Suzanne Clark, Walter Wangerin Jr., and George Young, and his wife, Ann, for their invaluable advice and help along the way.

# Versus

> *Versus* . . . came to mean *the turning*
> *of the plough,* hence, *furrow,* and
> ultimately *row* or *line.* —*Robert Wallace*

We hear his heavy kick against the stall.
"No rest for the wicked," the farmer smiles,

shoving back the door. The dark inside
teases the nose with chaff. It takes them both,

father and son, to back him out, resisting
bit and blinkers, showing the white of his eye.

Harness and plow attached, he stamps,
sweeping away the retinue of flies,

nods and strains forward at the farmer's grunt—
head sideways, feet rising and falling like pistons.

The harness jingles, the plowman arches back,
riding the stilts as the coulter slices sod,

casting it in bright heaps. The plowhorse blows
flies from his lip, small stones click on steel,

black sod turns over. His neck muscles coil,
slide, and draw his head in tight

to a flared red nostril, marble eye,
jaw wrenched and foaming. Meanwhile the son

dwindles behind the massive haunches,
jerking from side to side down the shining furrow,

until, tiny in the distance, the blade flashes
as he turns and starts a new row coming back.

Later that night at my desk, I still
breathe the rich humus on the damp air,

see that furrow stretch before me, moist ditch
rank with all promise, crooked line

starting here, returning here, forever.

# One

# The Newly Dead

The newly dead are concerned
they can't help us. It was only
a moment ago they were trying to clear up
some ultimate point, some elusive light.

They leave us with the other dust,
are gone, and we are here. Where?
Perhaps it's we who leave while they,
caught for a moment in a puzzling reverie,

wake immersed in the full light
knowing themselves and the place at last,
to find we have plunged ahead in time,
shadowy creatures chasing the shadow of a shadow.

# Cancer Surgeon, St. Mary's Hospital

*The wounded surgeon plies the steel.*
*—T.S. Eliot*

While I wash my hands, the patient is wheeled in.
The nurses help me with the gloves, the mask.
Skinless, breathless, I am surgically remote:
detachment is my viaticum and end,
more to be valued than a steady hand.
Already under, his face beyond the moons

blinding the ceiling, he lies, a serene icon,
comatose throughout his martyrdom.
Ritually clean, seven of us gather
like devil's advocates around a body
embalmed in the lilies of anesthesia
to seek and question each putative relic.

The sheet is drawn back. I take the knife
and make the incision below his clavicle
in one long stroke. The blood blooms
like arrows in the side of St. Sebastian,
carnation upon ivory. An unholy tangle
of tubes and clamps fastens to him

like a mechanical mantis. Its hoses suck
and quiver as I guide the knife
through swollen tissues. Slowly from their mesh
the cancer unfolds root by root,

a radical knot of cells insane with life.
The residents closely observe all,

watching my fingers move
warily over rivers and swamps of flesh
to cut the cannibal orchid from its jungle
and drop it in a pail.
Then with needles, quick and quick,
they stitch the suture to a neat half-moon.

Washed, swaddled in sheets again, he drifts
beyond time in the brilliant shallows
of eternity, his pulse rising like a line
of surf while the siren anesthesia
still calls to him from inhuman depths.
They wheel him out into the dim night

corridor. The nurses clean up. I remove
my gloves, stoop to the basin, the water
winks and flashes on my wedding ring.
Another day ends and I return
home to my wife. A meal, a few hours' sleep,
and once again these hands will take
up flesh to be broken for all our sakes.

*for Richard Selzer*

## The Surgeon After Hours

Strange how they visit me at 3 a.m.,
　　some accusing, some grateful, some both—
faces tight with pain, flushed and heavy, or
　　indifferent, anesthetized. They take shape
like patches of fog in my headlights while I
　　thread these dark streets home. They come
beseeching, pleading with me, though I can
　　no longer help them, nor tell them not to come,
or rise transcendent with resignation as if they know
　　something I don't—I, the technician hired
to postpone the inevitable. They rise up
　　like this one, the woman whose heart
stopped under the knife for seven minutes.
　　Later, she said she'd died and seen a peculiar light.
I don't recall her words, only her face
　　when she tried to say just what it was she saw—
that and the way her hand, birdlike,
　　flew over the bedclothes. I wonder,
do our brain cells at the edge
　　burst with a final energy?  Is the last
illusion more real than life? I don't know:
　　*hallucination* won't explain it, explains
nothing, really. The divisible flesh both is
　　and isn't us—that much I feel and more:
we are the whole left when the parts are gone.
　　Something surrounds us
we have to lose everything else to find.

## God's Back

> *I will cover you with my hand until*
> *I have passed by; then I will take away*
> *my hand, and you shall see my back.*
> —*Exodus*

Beginning with C in the dank school basement,
You taught me to hold a note on the silver trombone
With the dented gold bell. Out the window, grass
Rioted in the humid air. An occasional breeze
Brought its green smell by the scratched upright
Piano where you patiently struck C—

Your finger pointing to that simple law
While my horn wandered and bellowed
Like a golden calf after the silage of Egypt.
Breaking an aspirin tablet in two, you swallowed,
Struck the note again—
Nodding for emphasis while drops of sweat flashed

Falling from your eyebrows to the keys.
My second note likewise flattened, strayed
While on the wall above us musical deities frowned
In a pantheon containing the marble pallors
Of Handel, Mozart, Bach—promising no manna
To me, lost in a wilderness of sounds.

Miraculously I hung on for a season
As first trombone, slid back to second,

After another winter quit the band
To mouth notes silently in the all-school chorus.
Feeling guilty and relieved, I watched
The back of your shirt soak through with sweat

While you wrestled music from the air
Over the dwindling remnant of the faithful.
Now, hearing of your heart attack, I recall
How your hand described an elegant  B
With a forceful downstroke and two loops
As we stalled and wambled through a waltz,

And that day, pale, you handed down scores
You'd spent the night transposing. Even at twelve
I sensed our brazen wails and tinkling cymbals
Didn't deserve such sacrifice. Whatever
Mountain it was you faithfully ascended
Its god was overwhelming, the music of his progress,

The single note you heard as he passed by,
Struck you deaf to our tinhorn blasphemies—
Even as I guessed, when you played the Ninth
Symphony on the old, scratched  78's,
How it must have deafened Beethoven
To hear the divine tread fall again and again.


*for Harold Brunt*

# Blackbird in the Chimney

*Good Friday*

We hear his feet scrabble against the sheet metal,
trying for an impossible foothold. The wings
beat and beat uselessly in the liner pipe
that tapers toward the top. What intricate
dark way did he find down into this crevice
looking for a place to nest?  Some strange

instinct led him under the metal flange
around the chimney top where his kind pause
to chatter every spring before heading on
like punctuation scattered to the clouds
floating in a long sentence across March.
He's trapped for sure. Sometimes one or two

will fluster down the main pipe. At the bottom
when the damper opens, the sooty pair
will squawk and whirr into the light,
true to the old saw, *The way up is down,*
lucky their hell has a convenient exit.
But his is sealed—the only way out is up.

I unscrew the metal chimney top and search
with a flashlight a crevice twenty feet deep.
The pipe curves: I cannot see the bottom.
Meanwhile his every feather's and claw's slightest
twitch is magnified by the metal liner.
"He's here. He's right here. I can hear him"—

my daughter's voice comes up from the fireplace,
shaking at his proximity, delicate as his bones.
"It's only a bird," I call down to her. "It doesn't suffer—
not the way we would suffer. A bird can't think
that it *has* suffered—*is* suffering—*will* suffer."
So ends my conjugation, muffled in the pipe.

"Still—he suffers," she says, and for a moment
the bird is still. Then the earnest scrabbling begins
once more. I lower a triple hook on fishing line
again and again. No luck. But my doing something
helps her and helps me too on that windy roof,
one step from rotten gutters. Once, I see the gleam

of an eye and imagine I've got him. For two days
I climb up and down the ladder with ever more
elaborate schemes until the scratching stops
and I must tell her at last nothing will work.
"Two days"—the Humane Society says on the phone—
"A third and, believe me, it's finished for sure."

My daughter is growing up. She understands.
She doesn't want her father to take more risks.
Her silence matches mine now, holding, as it does,
the neighbor drowned in a river, the classmate dying
of leukemia, the jogger struck down quadriplegic.
Her dad couldn't help this time, unlike the time

he drilled through the kitchen wall at 1 a.m.
behind the refrigerator to make an exit
for the shy and unwilling-to-be-rescued

hamster, who finally came out for cheese
and her maternal wheedling. Or the time
he released the gerbil from the cooled-off furnace

after listening for his scratching on the pipes.
That one died of old age in his sleep,
a seer, having passed on (if gerbils can)
a vision to his cagemate of a cold
dark place at the bottom, an inedible wall,
hunger, thirst, and fear—when, suddenly,
beyond all expectation, the wall opened
and light came through and a warm human hand.

## Straight at the Blue

Her spine straightens by an inch.
Someone coughs, goes out of the room.
They pray again. Three days later
her shoulders lose their narrow pinch.

They pray every day for an hour:
one leg has lengthened, a knee bends.
Soon light registers and her voice box
limbers. A slow power

burns through her parents' hands. They,
father and mother, can hardly believe,
but the ministry of their hands murmurs
through the mouths of neighbors. Later

when she is whole, they claim
one closer to her than themselves has done
again what he did, but the world will not
notice in the fall-out of news his name

anymore than usual. Who can explain these hours
to legions of the reasonable and decent?
All we know is the healing love
of one tending her atoms like flowers.

Yet none can deny that the healed girl—
despite our offended unbelief—
opens her eyes, smiles straight at the blue china
floating toward her rich with cream and cereal.


*for Francis MacNutt*

# Fireworks

A few reports at midnight the night before
opened spaces in the sky and in my sleep,
and by the early morning of the Fourth
the bittersweet smell was lurking in the air.
For weeks I'd stared at mauve, green,
and red rice paper packets of firecrackers
covered with mystical Chinese characters,
contraband I'd saved-for all that winter—
round cherry bombs, bottle rockets,
whizzbangs, Roman candles, ladyfingers,
shipped in a plain brown cardboard box.

Behind Dick Leckband's house that afternoon
we blew up toy entrenchments, bushes, crabgrass,
whole strings dissolving, drifting down in flakes,
cans rocketing through the air over cannoncrackers,
rattling windows until a cruiser idled by,
its red light flashing like a Roman candle.

At dusk with cousins, aunts, and uncles,
we hurried to the park and the town's display,
spreading blankets in the growing dark,
waiting forever, dizzy with yearning, until
unannounced, except for a fizz of sparks,
a solo rocket cracked open the heavens.

Sighing together in a wave, we watched
pure silver scrawl across the sky, golden rain,

green crowns of light and red Ezekiel's wheels,
purple cataracts, orange asters, yellow fountains—
the whole earth blooming in the heavens
again and again and again while we gazed up
from the dark void at fire spreading out
in a recurring pattern each time different:
the secret work of gravity and light
by which everything came suddenly out of nothing,
fading back into it, rising and falling,
until the end when the American flag
unfurled and blazed brilliantly on its wire
down to a coal, leaving a sweet haze
we walked home through in the double dark
among the crowds murmuring like leaves.
Eyes, ears sated, too tired almost to move,
we stumbled beside our parents who were lost
in talk of ordinary things as if they hadn't
just seen the worlds created and expire.

Drunk on the lingering smoke and its fled music,
hot and sticky, we climbed upstairs
to the sheets glowing in the white summer night
where, scarcely out of our clothes, we fell asleep
to dream in that fecund darkness of the light,
the beginning and end and all things in between.

*for Richard Leckband, 1940-2002*

Two

# The Very First Dream of Morning

The sun puts in a slow stick
    and touches everything green.
        He hears the mosquito-whine
            of a motor grow louder, then
        a cluck and thump as it stops.
A shadow wavers over him.

He ignores the thin silver line
    flung like a spider's filament
        from a shadowy center again
            and again. The shadow leaves,
        the sun finishes its leap,
and still he hasn't moved

from under the log whose edges
    sway with moss. A turtle
        pokes out its head, pulls it in.
            The surface silvers, blackens.
        A yellow worm of a moon
writhes on the water.

Except for his flowering gills,
    he is motionless, waiting
        until sun and moon darken
            and the lake disappears in a mist—
        when someone, unprepared,
will cry out as if in sleep,

hands fumbling for the reel,
  knowing he has been struck
    (as the pole bends, pulling him down,
      and the boat nearly capsizes)
  by what rises from under the surface
like the very first dream of morning.

# Bee-Wolf

*Anglo-Saxon kenning for 'bear'*

By July he is legendary,
  rising, a shadow by the woodpile
after the last light has gone,
  to splinter the kitchen door,
gut the honeymooners' cabin,
  and vanish in a cloud of flour.

Two linemen trapped up a pole
  watch while he tears the seat
from their van, swallows both lunches,
  crushing the tin boxes flat.
At night we lie awake listening
  for his heavy steps by the icehouse.

At noon in the blackberry clearing,
  fingers red with juice,
we feel his small eyes focus
  through a green, buzzing slit
and sweat while cobwebs scribble
  his name across our faces.

His cousin in the farmer's zoo
  is an amiable rotundity,
swigging the red syrup-water
  we buy for a quarter, fur
hanging in moth-eaten swatches—
  tipsy, an engaging buffoon.

Yet unreconstructed, this one
  roams the Chequamegon Forest
and our nightmares all summer.
  In mine, hunched over his spoor,
I look up to find his fangs
  chalk-blue in the moon.

Branches crack as I clamber
  up a smooth trunk, fall with a yell
back to the clutching sheets.
  In one of yours, you tell how
he rises, coated with honey,
  the bees a black storm about him,

a shifting shirt of flame
  he tears at with his paws
while he stumbles toward the lake,
  golden-throated and singing,
blindly and in pain,
  of honey at the heart of the wood.

# A Dream of Feeding Pigs

Always when the sun, red sow,
gives suck to fields in the west,
I put on gloves to help my uncle.
Our breath ghosting white above us,
we climb the gray Ford tractor
and rumble to the broken crib

where the last rat scurries away
as the door falls open. Inside
it is musty with a secret shifting
of kernels and dry husks. We take
shovels—mine with the small
cracked handle—and pile the corn

on the wagonbed where it glows
deep yellow in thickening light.
Our tires cut teethmarks in the dust
as we groan and creak to the field.
I jump down to untwist wires
and open the complaining gates.

The sun, half-sunk in her wallow,
the clay purple between stubble,
we stop in the middle and call
to dark corners. Heads rise from shadows,
ears flap toward us. Soon the hogs
squeal, crowded like foothills

around our small gold mountain
blazing in the last light.
We take our shovels and scatter
a golden hail upon them. Bright
ingots thump down. The hogs
grunt and snap at the cobs,

grab one and run a few yards
until all lie stripped on the clay
among dark mouths gleaning
the occasional tiny kernel.
We scrape out husks and leavings.
The sun sinks. The munching and snuffling

cease. Dark shapes drift away.
I stretch out on the empty flatbed
as it bangs and shivers to the barn.
Here and there on the floor of heaven
something small and gold breaks out.
Spread-eagled on that rocking floor

I close my eyes and open
my mouth to receive it:
it is falling,
                    falling in a golden rain
that passes through my body like the stars
collapsing again to the center.

36

# Mowing

The tractor floats back and forth
  as the green sea of hay wavers upward
in the merciless heat of the day.
  At each corner the blades rise and flash
while the tractor circles in its dust.
  My uncle, half-turned on the seat, watches
the sliding teeth eat his field,

his eyes above his dust-mask intent
  on judging the edge of the cut,
his hand jogging on the wheel.
  Sweet timothy bends and falls,
white and red clover, goldenrod,
  thistle—lights of a green city
where nightlong music stammers.

At each swath the field is browner.
  A rabbit bolts, zigs back to the thicket
shrinking under metal teeth
  which bite and are never still.
A fox freezes, slinks to the ditch.
  Blue fumes from the tractor climb
a rickety ladder of heat.

Snakes and gophers feel the ground
  vibrate deep in their holes—
in the moon will come up to find
  the sky crosshatched, nailed down
over them with stars. The singers

that flew or crawled through the wreckage
to a green field beyond the fence,

all night to a ramshackle music
  will sing of the dust rising up
and tell, while the moon grows whiter
  and stars fly like pollen grains,
of the intolerable harvest
  when the thin green grass stood up

in a chattering line
  over teeth strict and even,
and lay down in the face of heaven.

## The Cow Burns

The cow burns
 black and white
  on water

green and white
 with cloud, with leaf,
  a mirror still

as they are still,
 a mind resting
  on the thing itself.

The cow burns
 in shade, in sun,
  her amber eye

dreaming over
 the slow omega
  of her mouth.

Her udder swells
 as she crops the grass
  and stares at me

walking, an upright thing
 not fixed to the earth,
  whose dreams fly

beyond the visible,
　　whose mornings and afternoons
　　　　cannot be

chewed to a sweet cud
　　or squeezed
　　　　musically into a pail

like the thick,
　　steaming, simple
　　　　fact of cream.

# Red Wings

Moving through rainbows
that spooled out from our boots
across the oily water,
we walked the cattail swamp
watching for telltale wrigglers,
larvae, hatched and ready
to put on wings and plague

the suburban twilight.
Our waders cooled
as water pressed around them
and sharp cattail leaves
scraped tiny acid trails
across our arms
to itch in the yellow noon.

The swale's vegetable rot
stewing about us, we kicked
up clouds as we lurched
in a green stupor
into the dazzle of sun
warping on water.
A cry sharp as a reed

split the ear.
                We looked up
where a blackbird rising
ignited the tips of leaves,

laying a fire in the heart
to burn unnoticed all year,
smouldering like peat in a bog,
underground, sweet and dark.

## Spinning

The water is low and smells
  of fish and dark-brown weeds.
The boat gives under my step,

sliding out from the pier
  toward the center. Lily pads
hiss lightly against the bottom.

Taking my spinning rod
  and spoon I prepare to fish.
The oars swing aimlessly.

Two dragonflies hang in air
  mirroring each other and the bright
hackles in my box. The sky

turns a slow circle over me.
  Without a ripple, the lake,
a single eye gazing upward

at all that rests on the surface,
  takes to its heart, tree, cloud,
and the quick outlines of my boat.

For a moment the horizon
  focuses on this place
where I stretch out a thin line

and, thoughtless, draw it in,
  turning as the woods turn with me.
I toss out the silver spoon

over and over, not caring
  what it takes from the deep
root-colored water, knowing only

that a wavery image is written
  on the sky caught in the water
of a boat, a face, and an arm

casting something bright to the clouds
  and reeling in silver. Again
I fling it out, and again,

spinning from the center of the world.

# Sunfish

Branches leafless and wet,
  a scrim of snow hissing
over a sheet-metal surface,
  the three of us rock in a boat
with a three-and-a-half horse outboard
  across the lake in May.

My father's sweater, too large,
  scratches my neck as I stare
down at the green thwart, smell
  the fishy rain and the dull
rainbow slosh of the bilge
  swinging through each wave-trough.

Out of the wind at last,
  the motor clucks, stops.
My grandfather takes the oars,
  his cigar unlit, straight out,
his face stiffening around it
  in a meditative glaze.

My hands too numb to feel
  the line beneath my thumb,
I cast the red-and-white streamer
  under three beads of lead
and let it roll, feeling the slight
  bend of the long metal rod.

Soon at the electric tug
 I lift silver from the waters
the flat, prickly-finned sunfish
 broad as an iron. My father
unhooks and strings it with the others
 in an astonished choir.

Fish after fish, they come
 until we have fifty or sixty.
I stay warm with the knowledge
 that the next bite will come,
my hands sweet with fish-slime, snow
 dissolving on the surface.

Now wet to the neck, numb,
 we pull into the pier,
our legs prickly, unsteady.
 Stooping, I lift the catch,
small dull moons rising together,
 a necklace of silver coins,

and pour them like change in the livebox.
 Limping with cold to the cabin,
we crawl under blankets where fire
 swims all night in the logs—
the red gills breathing
 in and out, in and out, the fins
wavering blue, wavering gold.

*for FWS*

46

# Connection

Lying on the edge of the boat,
watching my face in the water
fall apart and reassemble
in the long, graded light,
trailing one hand and my plug,
its last hook skimming the surface,

I watch the reflected clouds
blow through me while the birches
sway along the shore,
twisting shapes white and green,
and so don't see the dark
shadow under me rise,

lunge at the bait and vanish
as bubbles at the surface
spin on the eddy. I am
awake too late to his presence,
straighten and toss the lure
in a high arc to where he must be.

With a feverish sputter
the yellow plug flashes in the sun,
raises a commotion. Yet
I know all this is an act
of false hope and adrenalin,
a charade fishermen act out

after the moment is past.
He will not come back now
to me, stiff, intent.
Later under a cloudy moon,
perhaps—while I watch my shadow
climb and sink on the water,

listen to the thirsty whine
of mosquitoes gathering in hordes,
and sweat, glued to the thwart,
half-asleep from the boat's slight rocking
as it floats by inches to shore
over wavering black pines—

will his lightning strike my thumb
from the reel and the lake come alive
under the tilting boat.
Only then will I know,
while the dark mouth struggles with my line,
that for once I have really connected

(at the moment I didn't care,
drifting light as a feather)
with the waters under the earth.

# Canoe at Evening

On the mirror-still water, its widening vee
covering the lake's enormous vowel,
our canoe glides out from shore.

Each eddy slows and flattens. Only a tremor
reveals where we have been. In our wake
a loon trolls, moths flirt and dip,

waterbugs scribble and vanish. A deep
pink spreads in the west, the firetower
black against it and the first white

flakes of stars. We pull over narrow shoals
past an empty float into the shadow
of the Jameses' shore. Abandoned birches

double themselves on the water.
We talk of many things, hanging there
in a green twilight between two heavens.

A loon's laugh shakes from the darkness
gathering behind Vicker's Point. We turn
and once again crease the salmon-tinted bay,

paddles rising and flashing
toward the cabin, whose red lamps blink
through flickering caves of leaves.

Easing the canoe on shore, we walk uphill,
partridge-berries nodding against our ankles,
leaving the lake to itself,

the loon's indecipherable laughter,
and stars that rise to the surface
like fry to shimmer and feed.


*for LCS*

## Loon

As if in sleep I hear
the buried cry,
white breath of the lake

revolving across water,
cold as the dawn moon
or the fish numb in my hands.

Hollow from the swamp it rolls,
a grieving ghost,
hovers over the bay

rebounding from the rocks
and icy lip of the lake,
from stiffening branches

and bloodless leaves.
Tremolo in the clouds,
its echo fades

over the edge of the world—
uttering the lake's heart
in an ultimate vowel.

# The Hunter

Orion walks again, the night
black and moist with leaves,
chill with the buried smells
rising from wet grass. The earth
tilts once more toward this hunter,
again offering him what

he has not found, though he never
increases nor slackens his pace.
The cartridges in his belt
burnish bright as ever,
the long barrel hanging down
gleams with blueing. He breathes

the cold promise of autumn
which each year lifts his heart
to fields of unseen game
beyond the glittering leaves
and thickets of stars.
Shouldering the moon he climbs

half a hemisphere. Yet
always at the instant he closes
the azimuth of desire,
the world turns and he falls,
fading in the gradual light
that blots him from the sky.

Still, each dusk he returns—
chalk points on a board,
a map, an ancient circuit
imprinted on the skull,
mirroring the shape of the heavens.
His body wrapped in night,

his face shadowed by stars,
he places one foot on the sky,
stalking his quarry forever.

## Weather Report

The snow in North Dakota asks a question
with no question mark, no capital letter,
to indicate where it begins and ends
or what lies in the middle, for that matter.
The question is white and drifts above the cab
of the snowplow while in its orange light
people lean into the wind along the curb,
digging out cars that vanish in the night.

At home their dogs are silent, hearing no sound.
The cattle huddle and freeze, and buffalo
crossing the buried fence, free now to roam,
stand silver and stiff as nickels in the dawn—
eyes frozen wide and blank as if they tried
to comprehend the question while they died.

# The Snow Falls

The snow falls with abandon, falls
every which way down. Each intricate flake
covers the scarred earth with its white coat.

How light a caress, this inch of snow:
it touches the trees, clings to the wires,
the dandruff of angels, a celestial worry

over all things. Now the mouse huddles
under leaves, the mole digs deeper,
the owl glides quietly, offering absolution.

The moon hangs above it, a cold query.
Sparrows circle from the chimney like ashes
while the cat peers steadily from the skeletal

shadow of the fence. In the wave's swell
a shark turns suddenly
unappeasable, a whale swallows chiliads

of krill. So the world groans and dissolves
into itself. In this darkness the thing happens:
lives become other lives, are cast up

for the moon's clear inspection, pox-faced,
wearing a dark coat and hat. Sometimes she seems
about to comment. The surf erases another line.

All this hunger and movement, this striving.
The snow throws itself down in pity
from the order of heaven where things are clear

as the horizon retreating from a space shuttle
or the edge of Africa, a calm and simple line.
From there the snow comes, an infinite army

who throw themselves down, wings and all,
in utter abandon. Each tiny hosanna
patterns the air for a moment. Each small

forgiveness lights upon the earth, dissolves.

# Three

# Levity

*St. Joseph of Cupertino, 1603-1663*

Simple Joseph, *idiota* of the slack mouth
  elastically gaping at the various world
made impatient men laugh until they found
 · his innocence of the law of gravity
allowed him to take his ease upon the air.

Aloft at the slightest hint of beauty, a remark
  about the sky sent him shrieking over the trees
where he hesitated like a cloud.
                                    Witnesses,
including a curious Leibniz and the Pope,
  are clear he said nothing important about flight—
left no theory—unlike some others who cannot hope
  for so lenient a sentence from posterity:

*Floating in the air in a state of delight*
  *seems to have been his sole accomplishment.*

## Sir Roger de Trumpington

In Trumpington Church where the cow outside
  rolls her sweet summer to a ball
of grass and sun and softly browsing trees,
  Sir Roger T lies brassed near a heavy fall
of light—a light in which both saint and cow
  lean duly gracious, one notch out of time,
in which the udder is as sweet to God
  as the horsehair's prickle to the mortified.

*De bon air,* in full armor, all his facial curves
  lead to eyes lined with laughter, hands that fold
in prayer to a *fleur de lys.* Beneath crossed feet
  a little dog tugs at his broadsword's tassel.
Nearly free spirit— a brass Chagall—he floats
  one foot in earth, tugging along the world.

# Tristan

The moon swung like a mace-head at his helmet
  as he rode, his mare's flanks hung with seaweed,
with sea-green veins, fighting the quicksilver
  tide for Tintagel. An iron wind sang through
his visor, thin grid of vision, of Isolde,
  of the steel mesh and winch of passion, of Mark
with the calculating look of a crossbow,
  and all those shipwrecked sheets tossed on the moon.

He half swam, rode, through the murk and welter.
  Huge pseudopods groped for him knowingly.
His horse rose upon a shrill of terror
  and crashed the postern gate at the last lick
while all along the water the sad waves
  held out to him the soft white hands of pity.

# Galahad

Starting out, the stars shivered and burned
  cold points on his armor. Transfigured frogs
blew their pennywhistle bagatelle.

The moon glowed, fragile as a tulip.
  Light as a ghost, he rode beside himself
to Camelot. And there all slowly changed:

all became stretched out and numbered. Any day
  might find him picking off men in the lists
or learning a score to please a girlish whim.

Soon came the occasional crack about the Grail
  from those only too glad to see him gone.
Others had failed, he might as well.

Departing, leaves tapped him with dead fingers—
  the moon a chink for any lucky arrow.

## A Notable Failure

He never went abroad to broaden him
and though he learned to read, he did not write
anything worth saving. Once, at a whim,
he scribbled something they hadn't gotten right

in the sand and erased it. Few could know
whether to credit any of the vulgar rumors
surrounding his birth in a shed. There were low
whispers and a gap of thirty years.

Then more rumors trickled through the countryside
about the artisan's son turned wonderworker:
probably a charlatan—blasphemer to be sure. Wide-
eyed, some claimed he raised the dead (and healed *lepers!*),
before the Romans nailed him—as they nailed all such—
and the neighbors sniffed, "He didn't come to much!"

# Annunciation

She didn't notice at first the air had changed.
She didn't, because she had no expectation
except the moment and what she was doing, absorbed
in it without the slightest reservation.

Things grew brighter, more distinct, themselves,
in a way beyond explaining. This was her home,
yet somehow things grew more homelike. Jars on the shelves
gleamed sharply: tomatoes, peaches, even the crumbs

on the table grew heavy with meaning and a sure repose
as if they were forever. When at last she saw
from the corner of her eye the gold fringe of his robe
she felt no fear, only a glad awe,

the Word already deep inside her as she replied
yes to that she'd chosen all her life.

# The Prodigal

She floated before him like a summer cloud,
pink and white through his sweat and then lay down
squealing, by her sucklings, a teat for each mouth.
The husks caught in his throat. If he'd only known
the pigs would have it better than he, he never . . .
*He, ripe offal, stuck in the world's latrine!*
—so he told himself over and over and over
and over again. With tears came a keen

ache in his chest. Next day he started home.
He tried to stop his thoughts, lethally busy,
but at night yearned for the slops and warmth of the barn,
the hogs' contented grunting and homely stink. Alone,
he knew he'd failed beyond all hope of mercy.
He didn't even see his father till wrapped in his arms.

## The Basset

*A poem is a walk. —A.R. Ammons*

What I do not like about the sonnet is this:
the sense I get beginning to read one
that there will be a thought, profound or less
than profound, the author has dragged in,

sad as a basset in a be-lilacked yard,
who ambles out to examine with rheumy eye
all passers-by on his short street, regarding
each with a look long and melancholy.

About here the thought usually takes a turn
(or basset, that is—lugubrious metaphor!) to stand
and stare at me again with grave concern—
this and nothing more. And yet I can't
escape that look with its convicting chill,
my footsteps echoing each syllable.

# Walden Communion

*The New England landscape is*
*like a radish salad.*
                    —Lenaye Hudock

Comestible, comprehensible,
  heaped up in digestible portions.
Thoreau had eaten far in Concord
  and still this knoll
with its floor of puce-colored leaves
  under May's green mist
feeds the visitor. These trees
  map out silence like pins,
a faintly invisible gold
  breathable, drinkable
as we bite into sharp cheddar, brown
  bread, and drink grape juice
at Walden, my daughter's
  illegal cat under my coat.

Some kind of universe turns here.
  Each new leaf is a star, a wafer,
a harvest the golden grasshopper
  above the Boston Statehouse,
the plague of tourists
  (of which we are four),
cannot devour: the pilgrims
  from the Ganges,
the agitated throttles of bikers,

the hoarse voices that
rattle with aluminum cans,
  the lovers treasure-hunting in the bushes.

Thirty years ago there was little water,
  sixty years ago E. B. White despaired of the litter,
in Thoreau's day the trees were small,
  the train visible as it hooted and smoked to the west,
the ice cutters muffled in heavy coats, busy.

But silence has survived:
  the water is back,
the litter gone,
  the train invisible.
This intergalactic space between trees has survived
  all the calibrated limitations,
this silence of the wren
  whose brilliant plumage no one has yet seen,
this voice that comes up with light about it
  in perpetual astonishment from the blue-green waters
that fill the oval of the bay.

Here among the dim gray maples
  and the white paper birch
the cat scatters old leaves like cut-off wings.
  We finish the grape juice, the dark loaf.
We have not yet seen the cairn
  nor the model of the hut near the parking lot
where the Concord dump used to be,
  but, moving back through this gray

afternoon, breathing last years' leaves,
  we glance at each other—
the four of us—
  our hunger satisfied.


*for L., L. & C.*

# Looking for Mt. Monadnock

*She flowed into a foaming wave;*
*She stood Monadnoc's head.*
———Emerson, "The Sphinx"

We see the sign "Monadnock State Park"
as it flashes by, after a mile or two

decide to go back. "We can't pass by Monadnock
without seeing it," I say, turning around.

We head down the side road—"Monadnock Realty,"
"Monadnock Pottery," "Monadnock Designs,"

but no Monadnock. Then the signs fall away—
nothing but trees and the darkening afternoon.

We don't speak, pass a clearing, and you say,
"I think I saw it, or part of it—a bald rock?"

Miles and miles more. Finally, I pull over
and we consult a map. "Monadnock's right there."

"Or just back a bit there." "But we should see it—we're
practically on top of it." And driving back

we look—trees, a flash of clearing, purple rock—
but we are, it seems, too close to see it:

It is here. We are on it. It is under us.

# Hurricane Édouard

> *Le cose tutte e quante*
> *hann'ordine tra loro.*
> —*Dante*

*Édouard.* Édouard of the passionate winds. Spider
of clouds turning round and round, pin and web

over the green eye of the North Atlantic.
Édouard, of the French name, arrogant and elementally

logical in wind and tide, following to a feather
the unpredictable course mapped by warm ocean and cold sky.

Like a nineteenth-century genius who despises restraint,
leaving wreckage in country after country,

in love with the empty center of himself,
tangling with the ocean's green limbs

as she reaches up flailing from her tidal swell,
rising and falling in more than the moon's pull.

Édouard, disturber of gulls that shriek
and flap stationary into the gale to at last retreat

behind the dunes. Édouard, whose approach leaves
the waves depressed and gray to sigh louder

and sends the people scurrying like leaves
inland to cower under leaf-like roofs.

Édouard, from whom the whales themselves fly,
seeking the depths, from whom oil tankers flee.

Édouard, who brings the green night of himself
to shut down the day, who groans and shrieks

in the black night while the house shudders
and the trees writhe, who sends boats

flying over land, houses collapsing in slow cartwheels,
tears up billboards, and cuts the musical score of wires

as Beethoven broke the harpsichord with his music—-
flips the trees so their roots show to heaven,

then wanders away forgetfully over a mad keyboard  of waves
hurling the broken chords of his music into an arctic void

before expiring spread out, breathing his last on the keys,
like Chopin hectic and bleeding from the mouth.

Édouard, in whom trees of water grow,
for whom the ocean becomes sky in a grand climax of the
                                                           elements.

Ah, Édouard, if only you had waited for Frances.
what a turbulence of love would have been,

what approaches, vast stratospheric fendings off, and final
union and implosion of cloudy bodies, leaving,

after the shock and thunder of your meeting,
the crack of the heavens splitting—

blue sky and small clouds rocking in the cupped palms of waves.

## Primary Red

*You are every image, and yet*
*I am homesick for you.*
                              *—Rumi*

Red night of lips, of fuchsia
bowers, red pollen choking the heart.

Red of lights standing, streets blazing,
soldiers melting into the ground, red

of the sun burning down into itself.
Red of liquors, of lacquers, of heart's blood

pulsing through the wrist, of fingernails,
of nipples, earlobes, and secrets.

Red of high noon, and the last
thin thread of lips along the west.

Red as the dark thought on the darkest night,
red caught in the dog's eye.

Red as a skirt, as the hibiscus,
as selvia, as the cloven worm.

Red as the mouth, holding the only word
secret until dawn speaks.

Red as the utter penetralium
that all love knows.

Red as the lace slip, as the bikini,
as a kimono and Chinese lantern.

Red as the light speaking in two heads
together, the tongue

caressing a lip, the finger
opening a bud to a rose.

The red shaken loose by language
into the fire of contemplation.

The red star winking,
drawing the heart to the red planet

that swims down
to drown in the blue ovum of the sea.

Red of the bull flag
and the toreador's hose.

Red of the firetruck passing in the night
and the taillights of a thousand semis,

red as a gas pump, as
the waitress' smeared lipstick,

red as a Bic pen, as a plastic notebook.
Red as the roofs of Florence,

red as the monkey's cap in the Doge's portrait
or the pale red houses of Rome.

Red as a poem approaching the mind,
red as a snake's tongue flickering,

slipping into the earth
under a stone,

red as the retinal glow
on the eyelid afterwards.

Red—red as feet pried
from the nail in the foot of the cross.

# After Viewing the Bust of Nefertiti

*Dal primo giorno  ch'io vidi il suo viso*
*in questa vita, infino a questa vista,*
*non m'e il seguire al mio cantar precisio.*
                                        —Dante

Dear, you may not contest it: you
are beautiful as Nefertiti. True,
her nose, her smile, her swept-back eye
which gaze out at eternity
may not be quite as perfect, yet,
pity the helpless sculptor set
to render the impossible!
Likewise, if some reader will
reject my awkward verses' thesis
that you rival Akhnaten's princess,
the fault is mine: you are above
the clumsy measure of my love,
or anyone's. No matter how
skillful the hand that traced your brow,
the line would falter. You, my Love,
without her crown or make-up done
to please a pharaoh's humor, still
are beautiful—at the breakfast table,
delightfully disheveled, able
to vanquish all those others doomed
to be perpetually well-groomed.

Whether stooping among your flowers
or in more meditative hours,

the cup moving toward you at the rail,
a likeness of you will only fail
to reveal the *je ne sais quoi* that
grows where flesh leaves off—a light
Raphael released from paper, yet
beyond words startled into flight
by this poor pen—the shadow of one
who thought of you before the sun
was kindled, yet precisely here
and for this moment made you the dear
image of that beauty and grace
who loves us with a human face.

*for Ann*

# Going On

*Once I am sure there's nothing going on*
*I step inside.*
　　　　　　*—Philip Larkin, "Church Going"*

Once I am sure that something's going on
I enter, tired of mere ritual,
of liturgy where no work is done,
of punctual repetitions. One can tell
by the face and gestures of the celebrant—
or, better, by the others celebrating
this continually renewed act
of grace (invisible except where a look can't
hide the intimate and present fact).

I go forward, even though mostly summer
is sitting, damp and musty, in the pews,
to where a few in the mid-week evening glimmer
raise hands standing, while others move
to kneel where the priest lays hands on them,
often saying words better than he knows
to say. There I stay until the end
of the service—once more hear the strong love
commending me to eat that I might live.

And so I do. This church's architecture
is nothing special. There are few monuments
or memorials present here.
Only the window in the sanctuary has yet
embraced stained glass. The walls are bare.

What happens here is rarely to be discovered
in anything but the people—well- or ill-favored,
oppressed by poverty, by wealth, by having spent
themselves to no purpose. None is good,

in our first understanding of that word. All come
with a sense, dim or clear, that what they amount to fails,
the intelligence that tirelessly adds up the sum
of things in a clear system, sparks, falters,
shorts out—leaving us to press the mystery
against the roof of the mouth, to hug the ghost
once fused with flesh and still enfleshed in us,
until our spirit answers *Abba* and we know
by living contact what we can't deduce.

It is in the faces, and these come and go
like the spirit, which wanders where it will.
Even Canterbury's merely a heap of stones
until the spirit enters there and wells
in living voices, and thirty bishops dance
gravely to a voice beyond the chancel's.
Let no elegy hang here like the ghost of incense.
Rather, let walls tumble, altars grow wild—new
ones will be raised up in three days (or less)
of the sort the living spirit passes through.

*Note: The dance of bishops occurred spontaneously
a few years ago at a service in the cathedral.*

# Four

# The Cave of Sleep

He hangs upsidedown as if from the roof
of my skull—his wings crossed over him
like Pharaoh's arms, locking in a wisdom

millennial sands have leached and buried.
He is here by the thousands.
My light tilted upwards stirs

all to a dark hoodoo: ripples of crepe,
eyes like red sequins,
fangs that glitter heliophobic.

He detaches, drops,
in wild loops describes the light,
shrieking a high staccato,

reading my shape off the wall.
Switching off the lamp, I feel
the air stir as he swoops

close, and crawl out anxious
for the sun's sharp definitions,
the sky's bowl of consciousness.

Meanwhile, the effigy of a bishop
with his cope about his shoulders
in rigid half-sleep, he waits

for the night, when like an afterthought
he follows me where I toss in the sheets,
in the quick inaudible voice

of sonar, zeros in on my dream.
Eyes twitching, I feel a peculiar
weightlessness, my hands grow thin

and long, moonlight leaking through
as I hold them over the world
in a kind of benediction. Gliding,

I hear each small lament,
the mole's grief, the mouse's fear,
the trembling mouth of the grub.

I circle that chalky face,
the white zero, the bullseye—
and hypnotized by its ring

plunge, head rimmed with fire,
all night until the stars fall,
too faint to be heard,

until with a silent cry
I return to the cave
and fold upsidedown with the others

to share in a sleepy murmur
secrets we hide from the day
like dark cells clustered in a brain.

# Turtles

They have thought upon this log
since before Socrates
climbed into the light,
or Plato

settled for silence,
or Aristotle
brought out his bottles
and labels.

Each crawls up on a deadhead
with the other philosophers.
Dull as old coins, old helmets,
they do not speak,

but there are subtle
inflections of the throat,
and eyes, half-lidded,
which stare at a question,

and a mouth that holds onto
a conclusion.
Each day adds to their library
a reflection of twigs,

a silver razzle of minnows,
or a new shade of green.
Though their council is old,
no one has spoken.

Sunlight like moss
heavy on his tongue,
their chairman is still
clearing his throat.

# Spring Peepers

Listen, as the cries of spring peepers [a type of frog]
like ghostly minnows
swim this way, now that, through
the naked woods,
moonfish seeking their home.

The moon's pale laquearia
flash upon the water,
the peeping is more insistent,
a whistling tide.
The deep croak of the elders underpins it—

the lime green, the light brown,
the dark green bull with his red earrings
hidden in the murk.
This amphibious symphony
shakes the roots of trees and the nervous buds,

lifts them toward the hologram of stars.
Shrill notes rinse the hollow rocks,
cleanse the hidden waters
running where streams
suck them to the deep ocean,

The frog hibernates in the heart,
come spring, awakes,
leaps and leaps,
sending his laser cries into the blood.
We sleep with short galvanic twitches,

87

dream of falling,
wake to moonlight burning along the floor,
spilling over the windowsill,
and follow barefoot into the grasses,
our pajama legs soaking up the dew,

down to the edge of the lawn
where the rain makes the ground unsteady,
the thirsty ear drinking in
these arias, duets, choruses,
these nightlong operas, oratorios

of swamp and woods,
these litanies of ascending summer,
from the intimate, singing auricles of the heart.

## Alligator

I gather like an idea
on the calm waters.
My nostrils, eyes, surface

without your noticing. Then,
like the first dry land from primeval waters,
in an uncertain mist,

suddenly I am there, my low profile steady,
where you saw only a log, a bit of deadwood.
I am a museum

of the Triassic, a special effect
come into sharp focus, my smile
long and obscene.

Each square of my hide is mapped out
like a city block,
my tail curving toward infinity.

When I open my mouth my teeth appear to be
some huge joke,
a Carlsbad of destruction,

My jowls are heavy with secrets and my belly
drags like a rich purse.
Hungry, I explode from the sawgrass,

take the rabbit or stray spaniel into my exchequer
before you notice, so quickly I slide under.
Running deep, I am off

for other sea lanes, other tonnage, but first
settle in the depths a while, full,
the idea of myself

spreading through me from teeth to tail,
basking heliotropic,
the sun a tiny point within my brain.

But night comes
and my tail moves, oar and rudder.
A dreadnaught sliding from its berth,

I sail in the dark on an unknown mission,
Nelson toward the Nile,
or Yamamoto toward Pearl.

I steam with no running lights toward another
inexplicable surprise.
My decks are cleared for battle while I move

silently. When I open my mouth
my teeth are rows of cannon, port and starboard.
I carry myself like a big stick,

a log so ancient, watersoaked,
it floats below the surface sodden, stiff,
but writhe like a single sinew, a green bolt

of lightning at a simple touch,
going after the pig, the chicken, the crane.
I am a mobile mouth, I live to swallow,

teeth within teeth within teeth.
I keep the waterways open for commerce.
I have the smile of a cruiser,

the charm of *The Natchez Belle*
smoking and sparking into Memphis, beating
the water to a waltz,

silks and shivering torchlights in my eyes.

## Mussel

I am
tasting the ocean
one mouthful at a time.

It is a slow rumination,
a reading of incunabula
in my cloister

in this cell where light
fills me totally like an eye,
then washes away.

It is a sifting, sifting
as the animalcules make
a tiny crystalline circus.

I collect essences
while the Atlantic waits
for the Sea of Japan—

it is only a matter of time.
Meanwhile each raising of my shell
stirs all the waters of the earth.

The slow tides call me home
but I stay and savor
these identical moments

that pass and pass
in a still monochrome.
I have a single foot

and can make short journeys
out of this box,
its lid gleaming above me.

The myriads rush over me,
the small translucent beings
with their armature

and transparent tubes
swept by the slightest current,
heaped up in cities,

evaporated on a rock.
I close like night upon them.
They become my slow thought

rising toward that light which floats
over me in the dark,
spreading itself on the waters.

Soon I will be ready to leave.
When the light swallows me
part of me will hesitate,

hang back at the hinge,
a little bit of flesh revealing
the radiance of my absence.

## Silverfish

It lives in the damps of rejection,
  in the dark drain, feeding upon the effluvia
    of what we are, of what we've already been.

Everything comes down to this: we are its living—
  the fallen hair, the fingernail, the grease from a pore,
    used toothpaste, a detritus of whiskers and dead skin.

All this comes down and worries it into life,
  its body soft as lymph, a living expectoration,
    a glorified rheum. In the silent morning

when we least expect it, it is there
  on the gleaming white porcelain: the silver scales,
    the many feelers *busy busy,* so fast, it is

unnerving, causing a certain panic in us,
  a galvanic revulsion (*Will it reach us
  before we reach it?*), its body

translucent, indefinable, an electric jelly
  moving with beautiful sweeps of the feet
    like a sinuous trireme, delicate and indecent,

sexual and cleopatric. It moves for a moment
  in the light, while its silver flashes and slides,
    and part of us notices an elusive beauty,

an ingenious grace, in what has been cast off.
  As if tears and the invisibly falling dandruff,
    skin cells and eyelashes

returned with an alien and silken intelligence,
  as if chaos were always disintegrating into order,
    elastic and surprising,

as if every cell had a second chance
  to link and glitter and climb toward the light,
    feeling everything as if for the first time—

pausing stunned, stupefied with light.
  Before we, frightened by such possibilities,
    with a large wad of tissue come down on it,

and crush it until it is nothing
  but dampness and legs, an oily smear
    writing a broken Sanskrit on the paper,

a message we choose not to read
  before committing it to the water
    swirling blankly at our touch,

hoping that will take care of it,
  trying not to think of it—the dark
    from which it will rise again.

# Evening Wolves

*fiercer than evening wolves   —Habakkuk*

Round and round they go on about nothing,
on the platinum compact disk of the moon,
the wolves. Their howls revolve about
the nothing that's eaten your life to its skin
even as it eats the moon to a thin rind.
Each revolution of the sound has a silvery
quaver, a light dip and resolution,
a tremolo, like recordings from the Twenties
of voices sheer and faded as old silk.

Listen, the siren starts up again and circles
in its long ascent and decline about the rim,
its aria of desire and desolation,
a litany of memory and loss
and regret settled into like this broken chair
on a winter evening while the last light falls
unravelled by two flies at the window.
Cooling, they creep and stumble on the sill.

The wolves leave despair like a silver needle singing
in the blood, a fear of the blankness of snow,
of the hot slaver of hunger at your throat,
and the red eyes weaving a knot around you
while the fire gutters and you hear no answer
but a murderous vibration among the trees.

Worse still would be the absence of this fear,
locked in this cabin with yourself and the moon,
worse for the head lifted in ululation
to make no sound at all but a dry static,
the O of the empty mouth yawning, the vacant
syllable of the moon fading to a white silence—
no dark accusatory, no gathering of angels,
no judgment of teeth like a necklace of knives,
no unyielding jaws locked to your throat.
The last pain is the absence of all pain.

Just two winter flies, a jot and a tittle,
as the muffled clock beats against the silence
in the empty room, a jot and a tittle
against the solid glass
through which you might make a run for the river,
risking the swift analysis of the teeth
cleaving sinew from joint.

Better to be driven by the pack
through the trees toward the overwhelming sound of water
and, desperate, pitch yourself beyond yourself
over the cliff into the cataract,
into the thrash and thunder of Niagara—
risk drowning and a quick oblivion that at last
you might rise again, broken and absolved.

# Rat

Peering warily over his moustaches,
with a dozen children to feed,
he pauses where he's pulled himself from the rainpipe,
his stare steady  but not rude.
It says, his frank beast-like gaze,
that your house is likewise his,
that *mine* and *yours* are an elaborate game you play
as soon as you lay down a threshold.
In a twitch he's gone under the bush and you worry
about foundation holes you forgot to plug.

He is not inconsiderate or impolite.
He simply goes with the grace he has been given
and replicates his kind.
There, and there, they move like night,
faster than moths or oxidation.
At midnight you hear him rattle broken glass
in the dark rafters over your head
while the cat crouches, waiting.

He is neither obtrusive nor violent, this intruder,
and you may forget you've ever met him.
But one day when you've forgotten even more,
he'll gingerly carry away
what no longer troubles your memory:
even those little matters of dress
he excavates for, after a seemly time.
His tooth will not wake you, monotonous, insistent
as a clock for which you have no use.

You will be alone when he carries off bits of your shoe
or bow-tie, watchband or silk pocket,
and, solemnly, I swear you'll not protest
when he carries off the ankle-bone
from which the burden of responsibility has been lifted,
until everything you have is his.

Look on him kindly, for he
at last will carry you to a freedom beyond yourself,
out of the box you have built all your life,
to a sweet disorder in the dust.
There you may rise, sift, and riffle,
dissipate in the wind,
until you are part of everything
you didn't pay attention to while alive.

He will help you find what you talked about
and thought you cherished
until the sun shines through all your spaces
and you bless the water with your absence
and the air is your plain thought—
until all *mine* is *yours,* and *yours* is *mine*
and the words nothing.
                            Meanwhile
look on him kindly,
this ambassador from the Other—
adversary, beneficiary, brother.

## Mantis

Still as a silk screen I wait, I wait,

invisible, part of the furniture,

for the ambling fly or worm,

the Monarch just alighting,

the beetle dark under its armor.

On the altar of my arms, I offer up

whatever wanders by. In love

I am insatiable, will take

my mate's head in his electric need

and devour it, swallowing his body

almost as an afterthought;

then, absent-mindedly,

moving stiff and brittle as a tree,

go propagate my kind.

## Water Strider

He walks on water
with long, tensile legs
skates the surface of this element
leaving no ripple, no distorted clarity
never breaking the surface tension
quite at home in the sky
mirrored under him.

He is no philosopher
though you might think him one
where he moves like an artist's eyelash
delicate as a thought, a contact point
a synapsis
between water and sky.

The thought he embodies cannot be
translated into language
only experienced
in the languorous stroke
through oils
in the sky laying itself upon water.

From the side he is Fred Astaire
dancing on a mirror
making it look like air, as if air
and gravity never wed—
debonair, a gentleman
of equilibrious smile.

In the green and flittering shallows
a watery prism, he wavers
over the many-colored shadows, a kaleidoscope
turning the world in a dance
his shadow revolving
like a zodiac on the sand
beneath all suspended in the clear element.

He writes one word over and over
though no one will read it
before it vanishes: so clear, it is
transparent, his *tele tele*
that leaves the thing itself
before you think of it as *that*
before it is *that* and not *this.*

Though he writes his word over and over
he leaves no mark, not even a line like skywriting
to hang in the air an instant. Now
in the moment of his stroke are color and shape
a pattern light flashes around, a point
that vanishes and appears
to vanish again.

## Garter Snake

I am a line going somewhere—

here and gone.

You can't believe your eyes,

for where you see me

I have already been,

a sly dividing purpose

in the dishevelled grass,

an S that writes and disappears—

except when I coil to Q

and flag Morse too rapid to read

with a sound like a deflating tire.

Like an unsteady wire coil

I sample the air, sample the air

of its small electricity.

When the threat passes

I uncoil and shiver away

into a crevice

where I wait with a question.

## Slug

White, moist, orange,
I crawl up the cabbage leaf exposed,
too much like your most intimate parts
to be lovely, to be loved.  I weep to the world,
my trail a long tear, defenseless
from its beaks and claws
except for my bitter aftertaste.
He who touches me shares my sorrow
and shudders to the innermost—my pale horns
reaching helpless into the future.
In plastic cups filled with beer
ringed like fortresses around your garden,
your lie of plenty,
we drown by the hundreds,
curled rigid in those amber depths,
so many parentheses surrounding nothing.
You do not understand nothing:
the nakedness to the sky,
the lack of one protective shelter,
the constant journey.
Millions of us wither in the margins
while food rots close by.
Nothing is a light that surrounds us
like the breath of God.

## A Colt, the Foal of an Ass

Contemplating the dust he stands
in the direct unbearable noon, tethered
to the dead thorn. His long ears hang
down, twitch and revolve as the gang of flies
brassily land and bite and ascend
in a constant small black cloud. His hide
at each bite quivers and smooths out
like this earthquake-tormented land,
while his tail, with its bathrobe tassel, larrups
and swats too late.
        His eyes, half-lidded
in the bleaching light, are fixed and still,
his plain dull face perpendicular as a post,
his forelock hanging over it.
        He does not
turn toward the stranger who stands talking
with the two at the door. Only his muzzle
soft as silk and still faintly pink,
twitches as his nostrils catch the foreign scent,
widen and lift his lip for half a second.
        Then
lazily he turns to look, eyes glazed, indifferent,
tugs at the harsh rope once, desists,
patient with donkey patience, already learning
the rough discipline that pulled him from the grass
and his mother's side.
        Now, without warning,
as if he feels a tremor underfoot,
some inaudible alarm from the world's core,

he bares his teeth and breaks the air with a sound
like a stone wrenched and crying from its center,
harsh and grating as a rusty hinge
on which the whole earth hangs.


                        Later
there is a moment with a crowd roaring
in surges long and hoarse as breakers crashing,
cool green branches to tread over the hot stones,
and flowers which offer a brief fragrance under hoof—
one moment of all those in the years that are to come
of fetching and hauling for masters bad and good,
when he does not mind what he is carrying,
when a sense of joy returns, the early smell
of grass while he first stood, unsteady in the field
with a beast's dim sense of liberty.

Still, he cannot guess what he is carrying
and will not remember this moment in all the years
until he is worn out, lame,
until the hammer is brought down on his unsuspecting head,
his hooves melted to glue, his hide thrown to the crows—
when he shall return to this now, this always,
he continues to live in,
this moment of bearing the man,
a weight that is light and easy,
celebrated in a rough, ecstatic chorus,
toward his own fatal burden heavier than the world.

## Daddy Long Legs

I am a circle. My perimeter moves
in any direction—up, down
sideways, forward. My center
is the center everywhere, for I gather
the world around me where I happen to be.
It is alarming how quickly I climb
your khaki pantleg, then scurry over
the grass you brush me to, climb up a tree
though I seem to have no head for direction,
hurrying and standing still at the same time.
One of me is as good as a thousand, for I
meet myself coming back in passages through time,
matter and anti-matter,
monads and mirrors.
Though I move I am still here
and here and here and here,
my scurrying legs
the mere static of time
in the brilliance of being.

I appear to have no eyes, no ears,
no mouth. I am a single thought
surrounding itself, a singular idea,
an eye staring at the inside of the universe,
a pinpoint of light which holds within itself
the history of the Big Bang
and the revolving archangels of the Deity,
the Pleistocene and Waterloo
and the Grammy awards,

a singularity indeed
from which all flows and circles on itself.

I am brown
as a bun and a cushion button,
my legs thin as hairs.
Where I am, I hold all down
for a moment, then move on
invisible in the grass until
I am again crawling up your arm
as if desperate with a message,
as if to climb the air were no great feat
on invisible threads of light
to give some intelligence of earth to the sun.

A small Martian robot,
a space module, a moving camera,
a heat-measuring spectroscope
gathering the information of surfaces,
computing it and sending it back
as I touch everything lightly,
a measuring up
and radioing of it to a transcendent network—
my legs like the hair of Einstein
or the mad scientist's
or the movies where brains with beaks take over
and siphon everyone up until matter shrivels
and everything is just an empty sleeve
and earth spins away as a colossal thought
into the abyss of thought around it
and there is a vague hosannahing of antennae

and a chorus of small green blips
but gigantic thunders of imagination
and a pure gold dawn when matter reappears.

I am the careless aunt whose hair strays
over a face pregnant with black-eyed susans
and fresh currant-berries
with babies and poems that flew away in the garden
and a smile that dreams another world into being.
I am what didn't get tucked up when you were a child
and made a wonderful mess in the mud
under the cooking sun, the grass
bleeding into your elbows and knees
and the mud on your chin, the small pebbles
lined up and glittering in a row, your own sweet breath
as you moved things and saw them in a riot of newness.

I am a hot-cross bun on legs,
there for the eating, whose bones contain magic
like peyote
to alter the world. If you bite my center
you will never again be content with peripheries
or the long wastage of halls and the dim shores
of existence on the margin, but catch
the single reedy scratch of the sparrow
straight through your heart—
nor be tired from the hours of waiting and
the gray inconsequentials,
the violet of unfulfilled yearning,
and the fizz of desire,
the sad antics of the calculated moment

and the paper parapets of weeks and months,
but drop into the center
revolving slowly
pulling the world by you like a sea—
a strong swimmer
reaching out and pulling all things past,
lightly touching all surfaces,
taking everything and leaving it as it is,
rich with a word you cannot own.

# Grasshopper

Climbing up the stem toward the ripe
grain, he dreams about the green center

of the kernel while each leg winches
and cranes, pulling him higher.

A breeze comes and the sky wobbles,
the sun shaking a mighty *yes* or *no,*

but still he clings to the thin cable
until a shadow passes over and he

kicks free, flying toward the sun
on a parabola bending high

over the golden faces of the wheat
clustered on long stems.

He catches one, which bobs, shivers,
grows still. Again he starts to climb,

pausing only to make a thin music,
rubbing his hind legs together—

windharp, dulcimer—
in a field fat for harvest.

Together his kind scratch their hymn,
a thin sound the sun drinks up

as they wither in this late August.
At night the stars come out like cold

bright teeth to eat the world
while he goes low and creeping

until the sun spills its red light again.
Despite the random shadows

of crows crossing the field,
he rises toward the noon light,

rubbing his legs in praise, ready to leap
at a shadow's passing

beyond everything he knows.

## Aphid

Filled with the green ocean

rocking in windy tides above us,

he has fallen to this depth

with one mission, an avatar of leaves.

I lift to the bark this one who has

risked everything on the descent

to crawl upward again to those windy reaches.

In those floating pastures he draws life

from the ground he walks on.

In that place there is a motion and a stillness,

and singing to an unheard music

is a sweet and constant occupation

there, in that shining atmosphere

where green pastures give water and float

at rest on the air.

# Mole

I am a prophet,
my eyes white and sealed.
I swim a long dark sea,
this tunnel,
pushing the dark aside
with hands like velvet gloves.
I am a slow swimmer.
In my stroke I dream
of stars that burn through this soil,
each a soft, white grub.
They come one at a time
to comfort me, but
they do not shine
except on my inner eye.
Yet I know the sky is coming
here where the air is bitter,
unbreathable as ammonia.

Once I thrust my nose above
and was blinded.
I felt pulled out of my skin,
splayed and waddled
mewling on the grass.
In that light
my ghost was written down beside me
and my shape thrown on a stone,
anatomized and judged.
I could feel the badger's lips

tighten in a laugh,
the white and black of his face
sort out my bones,
and the fox's nose moisten.
The great yellow eye
above swallowed me
and I hid
trembling under a leaf.
Then darkness over the earth
poured down
and I saw the stars
like small white roots
like bright flower-noses,
radiant pebbles
sharp as the teeth of voles,
each shining to the other
beyond the soil of night.

Again I entered the earth,
the long darkness of this tunnel
reaching on and on.
The beetle's scarab is good meat
on this wayfaring.
He is my pouch
and the mouse's thin bone my staff
while I head toward that room
where the mouth is sealed
with honey and wax.

For I know what this dark earth is
that I hold in my mouth like a secret

while I dream and shovel
sleep aside from my nose
in this long chamber
and wait for the stars to fall
to their radiant kiln
and for one to come
through the fire
and touch my star-shaped nose.

## Snail

In the dark backward and abysm of time
I make my home
lying here at its mouth
taking a little sun or reaching
into the slick grass

carrying the stone house of the past
with me, its heavy whorls and convolutions.
I am shy if a stranger comes
or night or danger
and reach back in, trying to hear

words from the holy cave of my birth,
what the shadows said on the flickering wall
in the light that teased me forward.
I listen to my own shell
to the ocean of becoming

to the flock of moons that led us to pasture
to the stars that foamed on the shore
tide after tide
drawing us up
the long climb on sensitive foot

over hard shingle
and the myriad shards of the others,
the white cliffs of bone.
Inside this smooth-lipped sarcophagus
that has ridden the centuries

I read glyphs on the walls
  like the fossils of ferns
    that have said something over and over
      for a century of millions of years—
the curious bones of the mastodon

  and ultrasaurus
    that heaved up the sky
      then lay down in a puzzle,
        the trilobites that carried on wars
flashing coded messages

  from under dark helmets
    to die in a huddle
      under the cliff.
        I listen to each century,
its myriad events

  that have gone unrecorded,
    its dark hesitancies and reticences,
      all those moments which crowded past
        before they could be contemplated,
the questions answered and unanswered,

  the cries in the night.
    Here in my coiled horn
      I crawl back into the rock
        that leaked life in the beginning.
It is my oracle

through which the future speaks clearly
of what has gone before,
  my conch, my ramshorn,
    before which the walls shake and crumble
revealing the corpses in their mortar:

  the uncomplicated green air
  entering the lungs of a vireo
    about to be shot by Audubon
    or the terrible invisible bacilli
breeding in the blankets of Lord Amherst,

  or the one who lived
  looking from the second storey window
    and recorded it on seraphs of paper.
    (*Seraph/ saraph*, angel/serpent
turning together in the double helix).

  My shell coils one way to life
  and I coil the other way back into it—
    matter and antimatter meeting in a Feyn diagram,
      past and future the points of two cones
whirling into each other,

    weaving consciousness, the brilliant
  *funklein* of the present moment,
    where all is possible, all is known,
      burning nucleus, homunculus,
the utter penetralium of desire—

this cliff that totters above me,
this library I drag with me,
as I sign my path with tears
silver from my weeping foot,
this exclamation slurred on the rock,

this short word that dissolves
into the path of morning.

# Seer

*The returning honey bee performs a dance*
*to reveal to the others the exact*
*location of the source it has discovered.*
*In the dark hive, the other bees interpret*
*the dance by the air-currents from its wings.*
                                    *—nature film*


*Now imagine what would happen if he went down*
*again to take his former seat in the Cave.*
                                    *—Socrates*


Having   found   the   gold   treasure
of Atahualpa, the   place   of gold-dust   one
can wade   in   up   to   the   thighs, I   do   my   dance,
my   wings   and   legs    showing   precisely   its
    direction—the   candle-tree's,   the    one
    whose   gold   cups   spill   over   with   heaven,


        whose    gates   of   ivory   blush
    purple,   and   whose   every    entrance   is
an   opening to   a   confessional   where   the   soul
murmurs   and grows   drowsy   with   absolution,
    whose   royal   touch   covers   it   with   gold,
        there,   in   the   flower's   secret   part.

The others swarm around me in a fever.
The sceptics urge their questions. There is an edge
of  impatience,  of  anger  even,  as  the  zealots
ask  me  to  try  again  and  yet  again
to  show  precisely  that  point  on  the  horizon
    where    E l    D o r a d o    lies

    beyond  the bell of our  ordinary  sky,
the fields and orchards we  labor  in—to  show
exactly  where  this  tree  is  that  is  different,
whose  blooms  are  storied  lamps  breathing,
    like  Ali  Baba's,  the  seven  perfumes
    of  Babylon—are  throats  that  open

        like  the  fabulous  gold  lake
    of  Montezuma,  or  the  gates  of  pearl.
I  am  exhausted, and  still I repeat the  pattern
for  those  anxious  to  take  off  unerringly
    to  the  source,  eager  to  drone  back,
        bellies  heavy  with  plunder

    (so they imagine), freighted with 24-karat
until  the  cellars  spill  over, lucent with honey,
a  sea  of  gold  hoarded  away  in  wax.
At  such  times  I  wonder:  Could  I  live  this
    dream  for  one  eternal  afternoon
        w h i l e    l i g h t    s h o n e

blazing in the sky before me
and feel myself melt into it one moment
to which there was no before or after
but only an IS of wings—
and still come back to this dark cave
to fan its meaning on the wall

where the others feel nothing
but the current of air from my wings
and understand my directions only
by blind intuition—come back, wings
frayed, legs feeble, to perform
this small dance over and over?

# Five

# Carrying the Father

*for FWS, 1908-1991*

*Pater . . . Ipse subibo umeris, nec me labor iste gravabit.*
—Aeneas to Anchises

I

From here I carry him upon my back.
He is no longer heavy, though sometimes I
stumble over grief. In fact, he is

thin as the wing on an October fly,
seen through as if not there at all, but in
a certain light suddenly ablaze,

a transparent map of all my life.
He's here, and his voice runs through
my bones and through the roots of my hair.

2

We are at Gettysburg on the observation tower
of Little Round Top. He in his summer khakis
tells how the gray soldiers came on.

I am five; the trees are green moving ranks.
Later, in the museum he shows me
the yellowing jawbone of a drummer

and hands me in their green patina
musket balls dug up, a pyramid
still my paperweight. Like him,

these words are more than I can carry,
yet in a draft from the window float
from my desk to the floor.


3


We push open the door to the cabin,
met by a sweet and musty cold, the tick
of mice in the rafters. The electric lantern

shines on the black, shuttered windows,
the furniture sleeping under white sheets.
You crouch: a blue spurt, a flame

crawls up birch bark in the fireplace,
yellow, orange, a hand's width
of warmth reaching out. A stirring, crackling,

and the whole hearth is ablaze and roars,
the log walls leap and shake with light.
Outside, you open the first cream shutter

which I unhook from inside. Blue sky
drops in foursquare, the sun blinding,
the thin birch leaves a transparent

green melting in the May light. Now,
all windows open, a warm wind of pine,
cedar, and smoke flows through the room.

You hand me the cold icehouse keys and say,
*Open it, take the boat out, anchor, oars.*
*Tonight when the moon goes in, the walleyes*
*will hit and hit hard, hungry from the winter.*


4


Those sweltering days you came home early,
jacket over your shoulder, white sleeves rolled,
we walked to the air-conditioned theater,

through colored shadows entered the same dream.
Or, better yet, while the sun retreated
behind smoke-blue elms, we walked over

to the park where, far off, we heard
faint shouts and smelled the chlorine from the pool.
Down in that damp dressing room my trunks,

still wet from afternoon, coiled cold
around my shivering thighs. The fur on your chest
kept you warm, you said, as we showered

and waded the footbath to the flashing water
not yet streaked with overhead lights, pink
in the fading humid afterglow.

You heaved into the pool, rising like a walrus,
water streaming silver down your red face,
and yelled as you swam to dunk me—

letting me dunk you back, push the weight
of your body under water, light as I was.
You lay there, pretending the dead man's float,

then rose up with a roar and a laugh
while I fled, climbing the ladder
to the high dive, calling for you to watch me

where, reckless, bouncing on the edge
of that heavy board shuddering like a tongue
about to speak its first clumsy word,

I plunged headfirst into the summer air.


5


Mother in her white dress with yellow flowers
crossing the green in Washington during the war,
my sister and I running alongside to keep up—

always at the end of the eight-millimeter film
before the white spots erase the space
and time runs out over and over.

White dress with flowers that I remember,
carrying the summer with her, the sweet smell,
the soft touch, the words, the laughter.

In that white summer evening by the Potomac
she is the whiter center
of the picnic, the soft clink of silver glasses,

while I, running breathless over the lawn
on which I've fallen, stains on both knees,
smell the green mystery. She moves like a cloud

with flowers out of the sky reaching to me,
lifting me, the earth rising up, the grass,
with the shouts of children: *Oley oley ocean free* . . .

Every Christmas you showed this to us, Father,
together with the scene where you wave goodbye
from the Chevy window, the peak of your cap

cutting a shadow across your eyes. At the white
spots we'd cry, "Stop. Run it backwards."
And you did. Quickly, jerkily,

time and space knit together
until the picture was frozen on the sheet
hanging crooked, a wrinkle running through it,

while we sat there, wanting
somehow to hold the trees, flowers, faces
down to that very day, reaching out

in the darkness for what was always slipping
by, even as we pressed it to us
forever: earth too heavy, too light.


6


It is dark and cold, the high night sky
black as a hat.
Stars like fish swim as you lean

on the rake, now and then stir the coals
of the last few leaves, their heavy ghosts
filling my head, shaking a star or two as they rise.

A small flame leaps: a yellow maple
leaf curls like a fist down to its glowing bones.
In its brief flare your face is

orange, your hatbrim lights from underneath
and your red-checked shirt glows and goes out.
In the dark your shadow beside me says,

"Do you see the Great Bear, the Little Bear?"—
pointing with the handle of your rake, its shadow
arcing across the heavens—

"Those three stars are the belt of Orion, the Hunter.
There's his bow, there his feet where he climbs
up the sky, silently crossing it all winter."

7

In Florida, which you never liked, you fell again,
missing a step on the patio, breaking your hip,
while dizzy with Parkinson's, planting the *impatiens*.

Disgusted with yourself, you lay an hour,
until mother returned; then you calmly gave orders
to the doctor and medics as they carried you out;

over the next four years fell again and again
trying to walk, until it was a joke with you—
how hard your head, how soft the furniture.

After the massive heart attack, they found
no pulse for five minutes, but you came back,
disappointed (you said later) they revived you.

Grown used to your miraculous escapes, we weren't
ready when my sister called and said
you had died quietly, riding in the car

with Mother. The medics worked an hour
while you, no doubt, hovered over them, kibitzing,
floating in the too-white Florida sky,

telling them to leave well enough alone, ready
after years trapped in that wheelchair,
like Orion to take the sky in one long stride.

8

Father, I have just begun to carry you
toward the strange country of the rest of my life
with the household gods and the whole past,

away from the ashes and the smoking walls
across an ocean whose waves rise steep and blue
to the continent of the future, where I shall set you down

flat and weightless, except when you rise like this
from a small gesture, tine of a rake, or ghost
of a burning leaf to your full height and voice

and speak to me even as the light shows through
your flesh, and every scar on your leather jacket
stands out sharp and clear and your voice builds

as you say, *Do not forget the dark*
*dear past from which all the shapes come, the rich*
*drift and sleep of leaves over and over,*

*this soil ever crumbling*
*in which you lay the still invisible garden.*

LaVergne, TN USA
03 January 2011
210857LV00008B/76/P